Baron von Steuben

American General

Colonial Leaders

Lord Baltimore
English Politician and Colonist

Benjamin Banneker
American Mathematician and Astronomer

Sir William Berkeley
Governor of Virginia

William Bradford
Governor of Plymouth Colony

Jonathan Edwards
Colonial Religious Leader

Benjamin Franklin
American Statesman, Scientist, and Writer

Anne Hutchinson
Religious Leader

Cotton Mather
Author, Clergyman, and Scholar

Increase Mather
Clergyman and Scholar

James Oglethorpe
Humanitarian and Soldier

William Penn
Founder of Democracy

Sir Walter Raleigh
English Explorer and Author

Caesar Rodney
American Patriot

John Smith
English Explorer and Colonist

Miles Standish
Plymouth Colony Leader

Peter Stuyvesant
Dutch Military Leader

George Whitefield
Clergyman and Scholar

Roger Williams
Founder of Rhode Island

John Winthrop
Politician and Statesman

John Peter Zenger
Free Press Advocate

Revolutionary War Leaders

John Adams
Second U.S. President

Samuel Adams
Patriot

Ethan Allen
Revolutionary Hero

Benedict Arnold
Traitor to the Cause

John Burgoyne
British General

George Rogers Clark
American General

Lord Cornwallis
British General

Thomas Gage
British General

King George III
English Monarch

Nathanael Greene
Military Leader

Nathan Hale
Revolutionary Hero

Alexander Hamilton
First U.S. Secretary of the Treasury

John Hancock
President of the Continental Congress

Patrick Henry
American Statesman and Speaker

William Howe
British General

John Jay
First Chief Justice of the Supreme Court

Thomas Jefferson
Author of the Declaration of Independence

John Paul Jones
Father of the U.S. Navy

Thaddeus Kosciuszko
Polish General and Patriot

Lafayette
French Freedom Fighter

James Madison
Father of the Constitution

Francis Marion
The Swamp Fox

James Monroe
American Statesman

Thomas Paine
Political Writer

Molly Pitcher
Heroine

Paul Revere
American Patriot

Betsy Ross
American Patriot

Baron Von Steuben
American General

George Washington
First U.S. President

Anthony Wayne
American General

Famous Figures of the Civil War Era

John Brown
Abolitionist

Jefferson Davis
Confederate President

Frederick Douglass
Abolitionist and Author

Stephen A. Douglas
Champion of the Union

David Farragut
Union Admiral

Ulysses S. Grant
Military Leader and President

Stonewall Jackson
Confederate General

Joseph E. Johnston
Confederate General

Robert E. Lee
Confederate General

Abraham Lincoln
Civil War President

George Gordon Meade
Union General

George McClellan
Union General

William Henry Seward
Senator and Statesman

Philip Sheridan
Union General

William Sherman
Union General

Edwin Stanton
Secretary of War

Harriet Beecher Stowe
Author of Uncle Tom's Cabin

James Ewell Brown Stuart
Confederate General

Sojourner Truth
Abolitionist, Suffragist, and Preacher

Harriet Tubman
Leader of the Underground Railroad

Baron von Steuben

American General

Bruce Adelson

Arthur M. Schlesinger, jr.
Senior Consulting Editor

Chelsea House Publishers

Philadelphia

CHELSEA HOUSE PUBLISHERS
Editor-in-Chief Sally Cheney
Director of Production Kim Shinners
Production Manager Pamela Loos
Art Director Sara Davis
Production Editor Diann Grasse

Staff for *BARON VON STEUBEN*
Editor Sally Cheney
Associate Art Director Takeshi Takahashi
Series Design Keith Trego
Cover Design 21st Century Publishing and Communications, Inc.
Picture Researcher Pat Holl
Layout 21st Century Publishing and Communications, Inc.

The Chelsea House World Wide Web address is
http://www.chelseahouse.com

First Printing
1 3 5 7 9 8 6 4 2

Library of Congress Cataloging-in-Publication Data

Adelson, Bruce.
    Baron von Steuben / Bruce Adelson.
        p. cm. — (Revolutionary War leaders)
    Includes bibliographical references and index.
    ISBN 0-7910-6392-5 (hc : alk. paper) — ISBN 0-7910-6393-3
    (pbk. : alk. paper)
       1. Steuben, Friedrich Wilhelm Ludolf Gerhard Augustin, Baron
    von, 1730-1794—Juvenile literature. 2. Generals—United States
    —Biography—Juvenile literature. 3. United States. Continental
    Army—Biography—Juvenile literature. 4. United States—History—
    Revolution, 1775-1783—Campaigns—Juvenile literature. 5. United
    States—History—Revolution, 1775-1783—Participation, Prussian
    —Juvenile literature [1. Steuben, Friedrich Wilhelm Ludolf Gerhard
    Augustin, Baron von, 1730-1794. 2. Generals. 3. United States.
    Continental Army. 4. United States—History—Revolution, 1775-1783
    —Campaigns. 5. United States—History—Revolution, 1775-1783
    —Participation, Prussian.] I. Title. II. Series.

    E207.S8 A65 2001
    973.3'3—dc21   2001028516

Publisher's Note: In Colonial and Revolutionary War America, there were no standard rules for spelling, punctuation, capitalization, or grammar. Some of the quotations that appear in the Colonial Leaders and Revolutionary War Leaders series come from original documents and letters written during this time in history. Original quotations reflect writing inconsistencies of the period.

Contents

Baron Friedrich Wilhelm von Steuben was an officer in the Prussian army before coming to America. This illustration shows the organization of a Prussian army camp. Friedrich would one day organize George Washington's troops at Valley Forge in the same way.

A Prussian Soldier's Life

Although he was born in the German-speaking nation of Prussia, Friedrich Wilhelm von Steuben played an important role in the American Revolution. During the winter of 1778, he trained American soldiers at Valley Forge, Pennsylvania. Friedrich helped make these soldiers better prepared for their battles with the British army, the best in the world at that time.

On September 13, 1730, Friedrich Wilhelm von Steuben was born in Magdeburg, Prussia. His full name was even longer–Friedrich Wilhelm Ludolf Gerhard Augustin von Steuben. His parents were

Augustin von Steuben, a Prussian army officer, and Maria Dorothea von Jagow.

At that time, the country that is now called Germany did not exist. Instead, there were many smaller German-speaking countries, such as Saxony, Hanover, and Bavaria, all located approximately where Germany is today. Prussia was the biggest and most powerful of these countries, with a large army.

For most of his childhood, Friedrich lived with his parents in Russia. His father worked there as a military engineer who helped the Russian army design and construct bridges and buildings.

When Friedrich was 12 years old, he returned to Prussia with his parents so he could go to a school where students and teachers all spoke German. Friedrich enrolled at a Catholic school in Breslau, a city in a region of central Europe called Silesia, located in what is today southwestern Poland. In 1742, Prussia had taken control of Silesia from Austria in a short war that began in 1740. Before this war, Silesia had been part of Austria for almost 200 years.

Friedrich's father wanted him to become an engineer, like he was. To be an engineer, Friedrich had to be good in mathematics. The school Friedrich attended had an excellent reputation for teaching math.

After being in school for only four years, Friedrich followed in his father's footsteps and joined the Prussian army in 1746, when he was 16 years old. The Prussian army appointed him to the rank of lance corporal in the Lestwitz Infantry Regiment, which was based in Breslau. Friedrich performed well as a soldier, and he progressed quickly. In 1749, the army promoted him to the rank of ensign. Three years later, Friedrich became a second lieutenant when he was 22 years old.

Friedrich enjoyed the army. He performed well as an officer and learned a lot about military life and strategy. The Prussian army, one of the world's best, was very disciplined. Its soldiers obeyed commands and had to follow strict rules. Friedrich learned these rules well. Many years later, he used what he learned in the Prussian army to help the Americans during the War of Independence against Great Britain.

By the mid-1750s, the tension level in Europe was very high. In 1755, Great Britain and France were on the verge of war. Both countries had powerful armies and navies. They also had colonies in the New World of North America. Louisiana and Canada were French colonies. Great Britain had 13 colonies along the Atlantic coast of North America, and in part of Canada.

France wanted to connect Louisiana and Canada by building 13 forts, south from Canada along the Appalachian Mountains. These mountains are located in what are today the states of Pennsylvania, Maryland, Virginia, North Carolina, and Tennessee.

If this plan were successful, the French

would be able to control most of what is today the United States. The British were worried that if the French plan worked, Great Britain would have only 13 colonies in North America, located between the Atlantic Ocean and the French-controlled Appalachian mountains. Both sides fought small battles in 1754 and 1755. In 1756 the **French and Indian War** began. This conflict is also called the Seven Years' War because it lasted seven years, from 1756 to 1763.

Other countries also fought in this war. Prussia was an ally of Great Britain, and would help in the war against France. France had several **allies**: Russia, Sweden, Spain, Saxony, and Austria. Maria Theresa was the empress of Austria. An empress is like a queen and is the ruler of her country. Angry that Prussia had taken Silesia from Austria, Maria Theresa wanted it back. While the British and French fought in North America, Europe, and India, Prussia also fought against France and its allies in Europe.

The empress decided to form an **alliance** with France against Great Britain and Prussia. She hoped that France, with Austria's help, would defeat Great Britain. Not wanting to give up Silesia, Frederick the Great, emperor of Prussia, attacked Austria. An emperor is like a king, and is the ruler of his country. Now, four of the most powerful countries in Europe—Britain, France, Prussia, and Austria—were fighting in what was one of modern history's first world wars.

Friedrich fought in several battles in the Seven Years' War, and he served as an assistant to Prussian **General** John Mayr, who was an expert in military tactics. He was very knowledgeable about how to win battles, and how to use troops in the most effective way on the battlefield. Friedrich learned much about tactics from the general and became an expert himself.

By 1759, eastern Prussia and Berlin, Prussia's capital, had been captured by the Russians. With

French troops moving to Prussia from the west, Prussia was in danger. But help came from Great Britain and Hanover, another small German-speaking country. They fought the French and kept them away from Prussia.

Russia and Sweden withdrew from the war by 1762, and Russia signed a peace treaty with Prussia. In 1763, Great Britain's defeat of France in North America ended the war. On February 10, 1763, the Treaty of Paris was signed, which officially ended the conflict. In this treaty, France agreed to give up almost all of its North American colonies to Great Britain, which also gained control over India. Spain, a French ally, surrendered its colony of Florida to the British. On February 15, the Treaty of Hubertsburg, named for the city of Hubertsburg, in Saxony, was also signed. In this treaty, Austria gave up its claims to Silesia. With Silesia now firmly under control by Prussia, and all of its European enemies defeated in battle, Prussia became the strongest country in central Europe.

This fireworks display was held to celebrate England's victory over France in the Seven Years' War. The war lasted from 1756 to 1763.

After the war, Emperor Frederick the Great wanted to reduce the size of his army, which was one of Europe's largest. Having such a large army was very expensive. With the war over, Emperor Frederick decided to fire many officers to save money, including Friedrich. He left the Prussian army with the rank of captain.

Needing another job, Friedrich traveled to many of the German-speaking countries in Europe. Finally, in 1764, after a lot of searching, Prince Joseph Friedrich Wilhelm of Hohenzollern-Hechigen, a small country located in what is today southwestern Germany, hired Friedrich as his assistant.

In 1777, after working for the prince for 13 years, Friedrich left Hohenzollern-Hechigen, looking for another position. He applied for jobs with the armies of Austria, and Baden, another small German-speaking country in Europe. But the armies of both nations rejected Friedrich.

Friedrich still needed a job, so he journeyed to Paris, the capital of France, in June 1777. He hoped to work for the French army, but his application was rejected. In Europe at this time, it was not unusual for armies to employ officers from other countries. While Friedrich was in Paris he heard about a new war in North America, between Great Britain and its 13 colonies. This war, the American Revolution, had begun two years earlier, in 1775.

Friedrich became interested in fighting the American War of Independence. He thought that his experience as a Prussian officer during the Seven Years' War would be very helpful to the American army. Friedrich realized that the Americans, fighting against the British army, perhaps the world's best, could be interested in his advice as an expert in

In Paris, Friedrich introduced himself as a **baron**. Baron, like lord and prince, are titles held by some members of the European upper class. As a "baron," Friedrich received more attention than if he told the truth—that he was a former military captain fired from the army. Being a baron is more impressive than being just a soldier. But Friedrich was not really a baron. To impress people in America, Benjamin Franklin wrote in his letters for Friedrich that he was a baron and a "lieutenant general in the King of Prussia's service," even though both were not true.

Benjamin Franklin is shown here during his visit to France. Friedrich met Benjamin in Paris to discuss coming to America to aid in the war for independence from Great Britain.

military tactics and training.

In Paris, he met Benjamin Franklin and Silas Deane, ambassadors representing the interests of the hoped-for independent country of the United States of America. Franklin and Deane spoke to Friedrich in French, since the former Prussian soldier could not speak English. Franklin eventually realized that Friedrich, with his military background, would be helpful to the **Continental Army**.

Benjamin Franklin wrote two letters for Friedrich. He sent one letter to the **Continental Congress**, the government representing people living in the colonies fighting Great Britain. Franklin sent the second to George Washington, commander of the American Continental Army. The letters introduced Friedrich and recommended him for a position in the army for his "military merit." Franklin also wrote that Friedrich was willing to serve in the army as a volunteer, working without pay. At the time, Friedrich thought that if he worked for the America army and did well, he would be paid later. But first, he needed to show how knowledgeable and talented he was.

In September 1777, after Franklin's letters had been sent to America by ship, Friedrich sailed from Marseilles, France, for the colonies. Not knowing if the Americans would accept him, Friedrich hoped that he would soon begin a new career. After his ship landed in Portsmouth, New Hampshire, on December 1, Friedrich began trying to convince the colonists that he could help them win their revolution against Great Britain.

George Washington's army spent the harsh winter of 1777 at Valley Forge, about 20 miles west of Philadelphia. There was almost no food or other supplies. Most soldiers lived in tents and were soaked by the icy rain and snow.

Valley Forge

The winter of 1777 was a difficult one for the American troops, who were also called **Continentals**. Driven out of Philadelphia, Pennsylvania, by the British army commanded by General William Howe, George Washington's army was in trouble. Defeated in battle by the British, hungry, cold, and tired, the Americans were not able to fight again anytime soon.

Upon leaving Philadelphia, Washington searched for a winter camp for his army. During the Revolutionary War, the armies usually did not fight in the wintertime. Instead, they camped until the spring when warmer weather came.

Washington found a campsite on December 18, 1777, at a crossroads called Valley Forge, about 20 miles west of Philadelphia. There Washington hoped his army of about 11,000 men could rest and be ready to fight again in the spring of 1778.

But Washington knew his army faced many difficulties. The British occupation of Philadelphia prevented supplies from being sent to the Americans by land or sea. Since it was winter, there were no plants or crops the army could use for food. There were also very few animals in the area for hunting.

While the British army spent a comfortable, warm winter with plenty of food in New York City and Philadelphia, Washington's soldiers were short of food, water, blankets, clothes, bullets, gunpowder, weapons, and just about everything else an army needs. Many soldiers had no boots. When some of these soldiers were on guard duty, many stood on their hats so their feet would not get wet. Most soldiers lived in tents, not huts, so they were never able to get warm. The cold wind and icy rain always found its way into the tents.

James Sullivan Martin, a Connecticut soldier at Valley Forge, wrote about the hard winter:

> [Most soldiers lived in tents] and were not only shirtless and barefoot, but destitute of all order of clothing, especially blankets. I procured a small piece of raw cowhide and made myself a pair of moccasons . . . [but] the hard edges so galled my ancles . . . that it was with much difficulty and pain that I could wear them afterwards; but the only alternative I had was to endure this inconvenience or to go barefoot, as hundreds of my companions had to, till they might be tracked by their blood upon the rough frozen ground.

Army doctor Albigence Waldo, also from Connecticut, kept a diary about the condition of the soldiers, many of whom were starving. One night, he wrote about what he heard in the camp around dinnertime when soldiers had almost nothing to eat: "A general cry through the camp this evening among the soldiers, 'No meat! No meat!'" Even when the army was lucky enough to have meat to cook, it was in very poor condition. Before eating a meal with such bad meat, one soldier wrote that the meat was so thin and full of holes he could see right through it.

George Washington hoped things would get better for his army. He did his best to support his soldiers. He tried to keep them busy with drills and other military assignments. But his army's morale was very low. Cold and hungry, they envied the British, only 20 miles away in warm Philadelphia homes. Many soldiers began believing they would not be able to win another battle.

As the winter continued and 1778 began, the problems remained. Washington knew that his army was still in trouble. Shortages of food and supplies continued. American soldiers were still starving and freezing. But help was on the way from Europe.

Here Baron von Steuben is shown training the Continental Army at Valley Forge.

In January, Washington received a letter from Friedrich, whose ship had landed in New Hampshire. In his letter, the Prussian soldier introduced himself to the American commander. He wrote that he wanted to serve in the American army and fight "for the cause of liberty." Washington also received Ben Franklin's letter recommending Friedrich for a job with the army.

On February 5, 1778, Friedrich met with the Continental Congress. The Congress accepted his offer to volunteer in the American army. Friedrich then traveled to Valley Forge, where he would meet with General Washington and volunteer his services.

On February 23, the two soldiers met. But Friedrich spoke only German and French, and Washington did not speak either language. The Prussian soldier used his 17-year-old assistant, who could speak some English and German, as a translator. Washington used two of his men as translators. They spoke French to Friedrich and translated into English for General Washington. These officers, Nathanael Greene and Alexander Hamilton, helped Friedrich create a training plan for the army, which he gave to General Washington in March. As the war continued, General Greene became well known for victories

Alexander Hamilton helped Friedrich create a training plan for the American soldiers at Valley Forge. Hamilton later became the first secretary of the treasury for the United States.

against the British army in the southern colonies. After the war was over, Alexander Hamilton became the new nation's first secretary of the

Nathanael Greene served at Valley Forge and later became well known for his victories against the British in the southern colonies.

treasury. The person holding this job helps the president of the United States with many different financial matters.

After reviewing the plan, Washington was

impressed. He felt that this was just what his army needed. He knew the Americans badly needed training and discipline. He thought Friedrich could help. Washington ordered him to begin training the army.

The Prussian soldier immediately went to work. He picked 100 men and started training them how to be good soldiers. He taught them marching, **marksmanship**, discipline, and military tactics. From six o'clock in the morning to six o'clock at night, von Steuben trained the American soldiers.

The training went slowly at first. Friedrich's assistant could not always translate his boss' German words into English. Sometimes, when the soldiers did not do what he wanted

The rifle most used by American soldiers in the Revolutionary War was known as the Pennsylvania rifle. German gunsmiths in Pennsylvania and Maryland designed this gun. The Pennsylvania rifle was long, thin, and very accurate. A bullet fired from it could hit a target about 300 yards away. Such great range for a rifle was unusual in the 1770s. Other guns of this time could not hit targets so far away. The Pennsylvania rifle's range and accuracy made it a dangerous weapon that the British army feared.

them to do, Friedrich became angry and yelled at them in German and French, even though they could not understand either language. Eventually, the soldiers learned what Friedrich was trying to teach them. After he thought these men were well trained, he sent them to train other soldiers at Valley Forge.

The Americans began to believe in themselves again. They were starting to act like disciplined, well-trained soldiers. Friedrich also taught them to place their tents in rows so the camp would look more like a military base. He had separate rows of tents for officers and separate rows for soldiers. Before this, the soldiers scattered their tents around the camp.

By spring 1778, things looked brighter for the American army. George Washington's troops had survived a terrible winter. New supplies came to Valley Forge, and the soldiers had more food available than they had had in months.

The commander in chief himself was feeling happier and more optimistic. He felt so good that he even played a type of baseball with some of his soldiers. Under Friedrich's leadership, the army was also now better-trained and ready to fight again.

On May 1, 1778, the Americans received more good news. France entered the war on the side of the colonies against Great Britain. France wanted revenge for its defeat by Britain in the French and Indian War and promised to fight the British until the 13 colonies became an independent country.

Now, with a new, powerful ally in the American War of Independence and better-trained men, General Washington's army was ready for the next battles with King George's soldiers.

George Washington (left) shown at the Battle of Monmouth, New Jersey. The well-trained Continentals fought in sweltering heat and forced the exhausted British to retreat.

The New American Army

General Washington liked the way his newly trained army performed. The soldiers were more confident and more ready for battle than ever before. He gave much of the credit to Friedrich for his work in training the Continentals during the winter.

To thank Friedrich for his help, the Continental Congress, at Washington's suggestion, appointed Friedrich as inspector general for the American army, with the rank of major general on May 5, 1778. As inspector general, Friedrich's job was to supervise the training and discipline of all

American soldiers fighting the British, not just those with General Washington. Now Friedrich was not a volunteer soldier anymore. He had the position, title, and pay that he hoped for when he met with Benjamin Franklin and Silas Deane in Paris.

By the end of May 1778, the British and American armies began preparing for their next battles. General Henry Clinton, the British commander who replaced General Howe, worried about the French-American alliance. He heard news that a large French fleet of warships was sailing from France to America, with supplies and soldiers.

General Clinton planned to leave Philadelphia and travel to New York to join a British army there of about 9,000 soldiers. By about May 16, Clinton decided to march his army of about 11,000 men north through New Jersey, cross the Hudson River, and sail to New York. As the British prepared for their long march, General Washington learned about the enemy plans. On a very hot 16th day of June, the British left Philadelphia, followed by about 2,000 American soldiers. Washington decided he would attack the British but wanted to wait for just the right moment.

On June 24, General Washington called his generals together for a council of war. This is a meeting where generals talk about strategy and decide how to attack an enemy. Washington, Friedrich, General Charles Lee, and a 21-year-old French officer, General Lafayette, met to plan what to do next. Washington decided to keep following the British and said that General Lee would be in charge when the fighting began.

On June 26, the British reached Monmouth, a small town in New Jersey. Clinton's soldiers were exhausted. The 95-degree temperatures made marching very difficult. The British troops, wearing heavy wool uniforms and carrying 75 pounds of equipment on their backs, staggered into Monmouth, needing rest and

Marquis de Lafayette.

water. Many soldiers had died from the heat during the march from Philadelphia.

Washington's soldiers, who did not carry as much equipment as the British, were better rested than the enemy. The American commander decided to fight the British before they began crossing the Hudson River. Washington ordered General Lee to attack.

But General Lee did a poor job of moving his 4,000 soldiers into position. By the time he was ready to attack, at about 7 A.M. on June 28, General Clinton knew exactly what the Americans were doing and was prepared for battle. Lee's attack failed, and soon after it began, General Lee ordered his men to retreat. General Clinton followed the retreating Americans and decided to attack again quickly.

Like Friedrich, the Marquis de Lafayette came to the colonies from another country to fight for American independence. After arriving from France in 1777, he became friends with George Washington. The Continental Congress appointed Lafayette a general in the Continental army, and he fought alongside Washington at the Battle of Brandywine in 1777. Lafayette also stayed with Washington's soldiers during the difficult winter of 1777–1778 at Valley Forge, where he helped Friedrich train the Continental soldiers. He returned to France in 1779 and persuaded the government to send troops, ships, and supplies to the Continental Army.

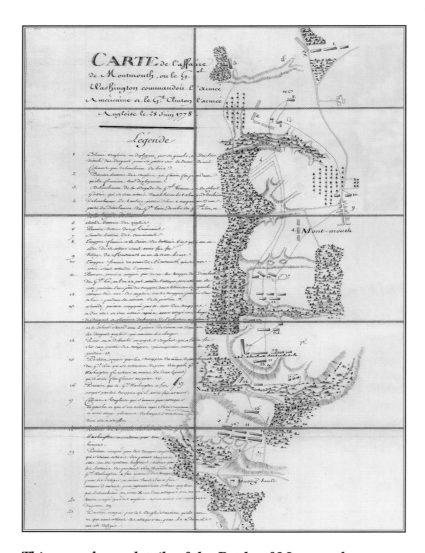

This map shows details of the Battle of Monmouth, New Jersey.

Now, Friedrich's training of the Continental Army was about to become important. The American soldiers did not panic. General

Washington stopped their retreat and ordered them to form a line and get ready for the British attack.

By early afternoon, with temperatures around 100 degrees, Clinton's army reached the American line. The British soldiers attacked the left, center, and right sides of the line. Each time, the Continentals pushed the British back. Friedrich watched the soldiers, and encouraged them in broken English to resist the British advance. Again and again, the British attacked. Each time the British were forced to retreat.

At about 5 P.M., the fighting stopped and the exhausted, hot, and thirsty British soldiers retreated for good. General Washington ordered his men to follow the British and counterattack. But the Americans were just as tired as the British. They could not attack right away. By the time the Continentals were rested and ready to move, Clinton's men had boarded British ships, crossed the Hudson, and landed safely in New York.

The Battle of Monmouth was over. Several hundred soldiers from both sides had been killed in the fighting, and about 100 American and British troops died from heat exhaustion. The Americans considered the battle a victory, even though the British escaped to New York.

Friedrich and Washington were very proud of how the Americans fought. They did not retreat from the larger British army. All of Friedrich's work at Valley Forge proved to be successful. Now, with a well-trained army and help on the way from France, the Americans began believing they could truly win their independence from Great Britain.

The Battle of Monmouth turned out to be the last large battle fought in the northern colonies during the war. In the north, the two armies were at a stalemate. This means neither the British nor the Americans could win any other important battles that would help decide who would win the war. By the time the winter of

1778 began and both armies stopped fighting for several months, the American Revolution was at a standstill. Soldiers from both sides wondered what would happen after the beginning of the New Year—1779.

Shown here are examples of uniforms worn by the Continental Army. Starting at the left is the uniform of the Third Pennsylvania Regiment; Washington's Guard; Second Regiment, South Carolina Infantry; Eleventh Virginia Regiment; and Maryland Riflemen.

Independence!

During the winter of 1778–1779, Friedrich was very busy. He worked with many American soldiers, training them to fight the British in the spring. He also wrote a book entitled *Regulations for the Order and Discipline of the Troops of the United States.* In his book, also called a military manual, Friedrich discussed the methods he used to train soldiers. General Washington and many other generals thought very highly of Friedrich's book. In fact, *Regulations* became the standard military manual for American soldiers for the rest of the Revolutionary War, and for more than 20 years after the war.

When the winter ended, Washington readied his army to fight again. In the spring and summer of 1779, there were many **skirmishes**, in places like Stony Point, New York; Paulus Hook, New Jersey; New Bedford, Massachusetts; New London and New Haven, Connecticut. While these skirmishes were fought, Friedrich was busy with his job as inspector general. He traveled throughout the colonies, inspecting American soldiers wherever he went. During his inspections, Friedrich checked the soldiers' equipment and supplies, making sure they were ready for battle.

Throughout 1779, the stalemate between the Americans and British in the North continued, so both armies moved to the southern colonies of Virginia, Georgia, North Carolina, and South Carolina. It was in these states that the next large battles of the war would be fought. Also in 1779, Spain became the second European country to join the war against the British.

In 1780 the Americans received more good

news from Europe. The Netherlands, another European country with a strong navy, entered the war against Great Britain. Now, the navies of Spain, France, and the Netherlands fought against British ships. The United States, which had a small navy, also battled British warships. In 1780, faced with so many enemies intercepting their ships at sea, the British began having trouble sending supplies and soldiers to fight in America for the first time in the war.

In November 1780, Friedrich became commander of the Continental Army in Virginia. His job was to train new soldiers, gather supplies, and send them to General Nathanael Greene, who was busy fighting British troops commanded by General Cornwallis in North and South Carolina.

During his time as commanding general in Virginia, Friedrich fought only one battle against the British. On April 25, 1781, he commanded a small group of **militia** marching south along the James River. Friedrich's militia skirmished with British troops near the town of Blandford, Virginia. Friedrich's men fought well, and for a while they held off the larger number of British troops attacking them. But eventually, the outnumbered Americans retreated. The British, who won this battle, burned a large amount of the Continental Army's supplies that were abandoned when Friedrich's militia fled from the **redcoats.**

Unfortunately for Friedrich, the British destroyed American supplies in Virginia one more time during the spring of 1781. In June, Friedrich withdrew his militiamen from guarding the Continentals' equipment, food, and weapons because he did not believe the British were powerful enough to destroy these supplies. He was wrong, and British troops, and **Loyalists,** colonists who wanted to remain subjects of King George III, destroyed the equipment left behind by the militia.

For the rest of 1781, Friedrich continued gathering troops and supplies in Virginia. He sent about 450 new American soldiers to General Lafayette, who was also in Virginia, in June, and then traveled to Charlottesville, Virginia, to recruit more men there. Friedrich was not used to the hot temperatures of the southern states, and he became ill from the heat while he was in Charlottesville. He rested in that city until August, when he began feeling better, just in time to participate in the most important battle of the war.

In 1780 and 1781, General Cornwallis's British army won several battles against the Continental Army and American militias in Charleston and Camden, South Carolina, and Kings Mountain, on the border of South and North Carolina.

In May 1781, Cornwallis marched 7,500 British soldiers north from Wilmington, North Carolina, to Petersburg, Virginia, after many of his soldiers were killed or wounded at the Battle of Guilford Courthouse, North Carolina. In July his army traveled to Williamsburg, Virginia, and

The British army, commanded by General Cornwallis, engages in battle with the combined French and American forces at Yorktown, Virginia.

then to nearby Yorktown. This small port city is located on the York River, which is next to the Chesapeake Bay and close to the Atlantic Ocean. Being near the ocean meant British ships could easily support Cornwallis, whose army outnumbered the 4,500 Continentals commanded by Lafayette, Friedrich, and General Anthony Wayne, who were all near Yorktown.

While Cornwallis waited for more troops and supplies, he built several forts and barricades around his soldiers to protect them from American attacks.

With Cornwallis and his 7,500 men in Yorktown, the British planned to send reinforcements to him by sea from the West Indies, where Great Britain had several other colonies. General Henry Clinton also planned to send British troops from New York City to help Cornwallis. With these

On October 17, 1781, Admiral Graves sailed from New York City, and headed for Yorktown. This time, he commanded 25 warships, which carried about 7,000 British soldiers. Graves thought this fleet would be powerful enough to defeat the French. He also hoped that the soldiers he was carrying would help Cornwallis at Yorktown. As he sailed south, he had no idea what had already happened in Virginia. By the time Graves arrived near Yorktown, he learned Cornwallis had surrendered. Instead of fighting the French and Americans, Graves turned his ships around and went back to New York.

During the battles of the Revolutionary War, American soldiers faced British soldiers, who were armed with bayonets, as shown here in this reenactment.

reinforcements, the British planned to smash the small American army in Virginia. After their recent southern victories, Cornwallis and his men were very confident. They believed they could easily defeat the Americans and perhaps end the war.

While Cornwallis waited, General Washington received the news that the British were in Yorktown. He decided to trap Cornwallis there and attack before reinforcements arrived. General Washington ordered Lafayette to take 2,500 American soldiers to Yorktown and lay siege to the city, keeping the British from leaving or being helped by land.

Meanwhile, Washington and 2,500 more American soldiers and about 4,000 French troops, commanded by General Comte de Rochambeau, traveled south from New York. General Rochambeau and his men had recently arrived from France. They marched quickly to the northern end of the Chesapeake Bay in Maryland, where on August 21 they boarded 24 French warships for the voyage to Virginia. The French government sent these ships from French colonies in the West Indies to help fight the

Admiral De Grasse sailed a fleet of French warships, which carried General Rochambeau and his troops to Virginia. The French troops were there to help Lafayette with the siege of Yorktown.

British. Before Washington and Rochambeau arrived in Maryland, Admiral De Grasse, commander of the fleet of 24 warships, landed

French troops near Virginia to help Lafayette with the siege of Yorktown. At about the same time, another fleet of 12 French warships carrying General Rochambeau's artillery sailed south from Newport, Rhode Island, to Virginia.

Washington, who was from Virginia, knew that Yorktown was located on a peninsula, land that is surrounded by water on three sides. He realized that if the Americans could trap the British at Yorktown, and prevent them from retreating by land, their only escape would be by water. General Washington and General Rochambeau planned to have the French navy block any British ships from reaching General Cornwallis. With the British trapped on land and sea, Washington believed he would defeat them.

The British learned that the French navy was on its way to Virginia and sent its own fleet of 19 warships with soldiers to reinforce Cornwallis and stop them. After landing Washington, Rochambeau, and their troops in Virginia, the

French fleet sailed again, this time to fight the British at sea after Admiral De Grasse learned of the enemy's plans.

On September 5, Admiral Thomas Graves, commander of the British fleet, spotted Admiral de Grasse's 24 warships in the Atlantic Ocean in an area called the Virginia Capes, which is near the modern city of Virginia Beach, Virginia. Graves ordered his ships to attack, and the Battle of the Virginia Capes began.

Warships from both sides fired their cannons at each other for most of the day. Many ships were badly damaged, and some were sunk by gunfire. But the British lost more ships than the French did. By late afternoon on September 5, the battle ended when both fleets moved away from each other. Admiral de Grasse had succeeded in keeping the British away from reinforcing Cornwallis in Yorktown. The French controlled the waters off the Virginia coast, so Cornwallis and his army could not escape by sea from Yorktown and could not get any help from British ships.

After the Battle of the Virginia Capes, Admiral Graves sailed to New York, where he planned to load his ships with British soldiers and take them and more warships back to Virginia to challenge the French again.

By the beginning of October, about 17,000 American and French soldiers surrounded Cornwallis's army of 7,500 men in Yorktown. Learning of Admiral Graves's defeat by the French, General Cornwallis began worrying about his situation. Now, the British were badly outnumbered by their enemies, and they had almost no hope of being helped or rescued anytime soon. General Cornwallis's men were in trouble. They soon began running out of food, ammunition, and supplies because the allied siege prevented them from receiving help from outside of Yorktown.

In early October, French Admiral Comte de Baras and his 12 ships arrived in Virginia from Rhode Island with the French artillery. On

October 6, the allies began bombarding the British positions with cannon fire. Shell after shell was sent rocketing toward the British. After a furious bombardment, the allied soldiers began their attack.

The Americans were split into three groups, with one each commanded by Washington, Lafayette, and Friedrich. Rochambeau commanded the French soldiers. As the allies approached the enemy fortifications outside Yorktown, the French and Americans were surprised to find no redcoats there. Cornwallis, worried about not having enough men or supplies to fight the allies, had ordered all his men to retreat from the forts that were farthest away from Yorktown to the main British position.

The French and Americans continued to storm the British fortifications. On October 14, the Americans captured an enemy position that was protecting the largest part of Cornwallis's army. After a successful attack by the French, the redcoats retreated, until they were inside one small fort. The British were trapped.

On October 17, 1781, General Cornwallis sent several British soldiers with a white flag toward the allies. When used in battle, a white flag carried by soldiers means that they intend to surrender. The British first reached an American position commanded by Friedrich, who discovered that the soldiers carried an offer from Cornwallis to give up. Friedrich sent the message to General Washington, and on October 19, 1781, General Cornwallis surrendered his 7,500-man army, one-quarter of all the British troops in North America, to the French and Americans.

While the British soldiers gave up their weapons, and marched past American and French soldiers, out of Yorktown, one officer from New Jersey watched them closely, and later wrote in his diary:

The British officers in general behaved like boys who had been whipped at school. Some

**The Battle of Yorktown, shown here, was a decisive
victory for the combined French and American army.
The defeat of Cornwallis forced the British government
to seek terms of peace with the colonies.**

bit their lips; some pouted; others cried. Their
round, broad-rimmed hats were well-adapted
to the occasion, hiding those faces they were
ashamed to show.

Even after the surrender, the British still did not believe they had lost to the Americans. Many were angry, sad, and embarrassed at their defeat and did not want to march out of Yorktown right in front of their enemies. But in 1781, that was what happened after one army had surrendered to another. The Battle of Yorktown was over, and the allies had won their most important victory of the war.

This was the last big land battle of the American Revolution. Now, the Americans and British began talking about how to end the war and give the 13 colonies their independence.

When the British army surrendered on October 19, 1781, a band played a song called "The World Turned Upside Down." These words symbolized what the Americans had just done. They had beaten Great Britain, which was considered to have the world's most powerful army and navy, and had colonies all across the globe. In 1775, when the war began, very few people thought this would be possible. Now a new country, the United States of America, was about to be born where Britain used to have 13 colonies. Just like the song said, the world had turned upside down.

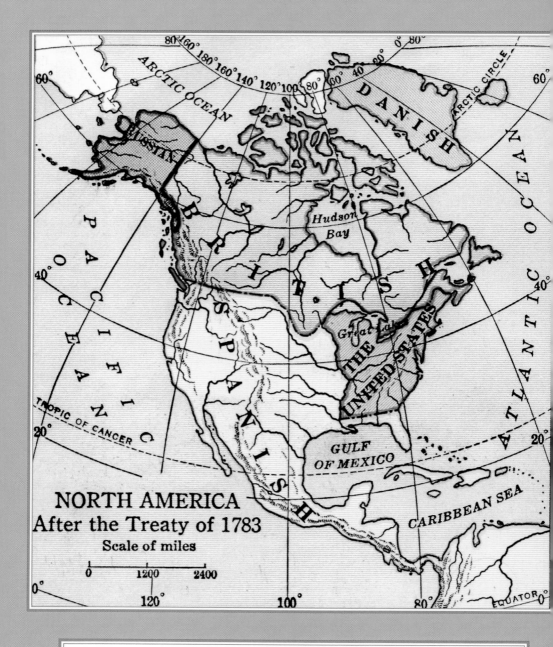

NORTH AMERICA
After the Treaty of 1783
Scale of miles

On September 3, 1783, the British government and members of the Continental Congress signed the Treaty of Paris. This treaty ended the war and established the United States' independence.

A Soldier's Farewell

After the Battle of Yorktown, both sides worked on what to do next. Concerned about the American/French victory, members of **Parliament**, the national legislature of England, began discussing how to end of the war. They were very angry that Cornwallis lost to the Americans and French at Yorktown, believing that their army and navy should have easily defeated the Americans. Many other people in England were angry and embarrassed as well that their powerful armed forces lost to the Continentals. Shortly after his defeat, Cornwallis, also upset about Yorktown and tired of fighting in North America, resigned his position as British commander in chief. In the summer of 1782, he boarded a ship in New York, and sailed home to England, never to return to the United States. King George III replaced him with Sir Guy Carleton as commanding general.

Parliament members complained to English Prime Minister Lord North about Yorktown and wanted him to take responsibility for the country's defeat. The prime minister is the head of the English government, and in 1782, was the king's representative in Parliament.

Under pressure from Parliament because of Yorktown, Lord North resigned, and was replaced by Lord Shelborne. New Prime Minister Shelborne decided to begin peace **negotiations** with the Americans and French to end the war. Peace negotiations began in Paris, France, in late 1782. The Continental Congress sent Benjamin Franklin, future U.S. President John Adams, and diplomat

John Jay to the peace talks to negotiate for the Americans.

While the peace talks continued, the American and British armies fought several skirmishes. The fighting was not over yet. The British still had a large army and navy in New York City. Friedrich, as the Continental Army's inspector general, remained responsible for the training and discipline of American soldiers. He traveled throughout the 13 colonies, inspecting the troops, and reporting to General Washington about what he discovered.

Although many believed the war was over, Friedrich and Washington wanted their army ready to fight again if the peace negotiations in Paris failed. Continental soldiers, the British army, and the French armed forces remained in their positions around the colonies, and waited for news from Paris.

By fall, that news finally reached America by ship. On September 3, 1783, all sides had signed the peace treaty in Paris. The war was finally over, and the Americans had won their independence from Great Britain.

With the war over and the peace treaty signed, the American army began breaking up. The new country did not need such a large army anymore. Friedrich helped General Washington reduce the size of the army. In the spring of 1783, Friedrich had also helped make decisions about how large the new country's peacetime army should be.

On December 4, 1783, General Guy Carleton sailed out of New York harbor for the last time, taking all the British troops and ships back to England. Continental soldiers and citizens rejoiced over their newly won independence from Great Britain.

In the Treaty of Paris, Great Britain agreed to give up its 13 colonies and recognized a new independent country called the United States of America. Britain also agreed to remove all of its soldiers, sailors, and ships from America. The treaty outlined the borders of the United States. According to the treaty, the United States would include all land from the Great Lakes south to Florida, and from the Atlantic Ocean west to the Mississippi River.

General George Washington bids a tearful farewell to other Continental Army generals and officers.

That afternoon, around lunchtime, Friedrich and other Continental Army generals and officers met at a restaurant called Fraunces Tavern in New York City to say goodbye to their commander in chief, George Washington. One room of the tavern filled quickly with men with powdered wigs in blue uniforms, carrying newly polished, bright swords and pistols. They had all fought alongside Washington, some since 1775, when the Revolutionary War began.

A table was filled with food, wine, and other things to drink. The room was quiet, until Washington walked in. The commanding general poured himself a glass of wine, raised it in front of his mouth, turned to his loyal officers, and said:

> With a heart full of love and gratitude, I now take leave of you. I most devoutly wish that your later days be as prosperous and happy as your former ones have been glorious and honorable.

After drinking his wine, Washington said goodbye to each man in the room. He was sad to leave the people he had fought with. As he said goodbye, tears rolled down his cheeks, and the cheeks of his generals, including Friedrich. When the farewells were over, Washington left the tavern and traveled to Annapolis, the capital of Maryland.

Accompanied by Friedrich and a small group of other officers, General Washington arrived in Annapolis, which was also the place of a special meeting of the Continental Congress. On December 23, he spoke to the Congress and resigned from the army. But before his speech, he wrote a letter about Friedrich to the Congress. In his letter, Washington praised Friedrich's skill, leadership, and bravery. He commended the Prussian officer for his "faithful and meritorious Services" to the new country.

In March 1784, Friedrich, like so many other officers and soldiers, resigned from the American army, and retired. He decided to stay in the United States instead of returning to Europe. He moved into an enormous house in New York City, called 'The Louvre,' named after the famous French palace in Paris. Friedrich expected the Congress to award him a generous pension for his services to the United States. A pension is an amount of money people live on after they retire and stop working.

But Friedrich was disappointed in September 1785 when Congress gave him much less money than he expected. With so little money, Friedrich could not afford to live in a big house anymore. He moved out of The Louvre, and into a small hotel in the Wall Street area of New York City. Saddened because his new country did not seem to appreciate all he had done during the war, Friedrich worried about what he would do next.

By 1788, he had almost run out of money when two friends from the war, Alexander Hamilton and Benjamin Walker, helped their former comrade. In 1789, Hamilton, the new secretary of the treasury, and the new president of the United States, George Washington, helped Friedrich even more. Following their advice, Friedrich sent another pension request to the U.S. Congress in August 1789. Washington and Hamilton asked Congress to award Friedrich a generous amount of money for his service to the country. Congress agreed, and in May 1790, gave Friedrich an annual pension of $2,500, which was a large amount of money at that time.

Although the $2,500 was still less than Friedrich expected, it was enough money to allow Friedrich to live a comfortable life. He decided to build a log cabin on 16,000 acres of land that New York State had given him in 1786. The state gave Friedrich this land, which was near the town of Utica, in appreciation for his wartime service to the United States.

From 1790 to 1794, Friedrich lived most of each year in New York City. But in the summer, he moved north to Utica and lived in his log cabin, which he enjoyed very much. In May 1794, Friedrich left New York City and moved into his log cabin for the rest of his life.

On November 29, 1794, about two months

**Friedrich lived in a log cabin, such as the one shown in
this painting by F. F. Palmer, in Utica, New York.**

after his 64th birthday, Friedrich died unexpect-
edly from a stroke. The next day, the former
general's body was wrapped in a fancy military

cloak, and buried on his 16,000-acre estate. Since Friedrich never married and had no family in the United States, he decided to give his land and cabin to his former assistants during the war, William North and Benjamin Walker.

Friedrich Wilhelm von Steuben played a very important role in the American Revolution. Using Prussian and European methods of training, discipline, and military strategy, he prepared the Continental Army to fight the British. His valuable help at Valley Forge in 1778 contributed to America gaining its independence and becoming a new country. Although he was a foreigner when he first reached the colonies in

Besides Friedrich and the Marquis de Lafayette, many other Europeans fought with Americans against Great Britain. Tadeusz (Thaddeus) Kosciusko came from Poland in 1776. When General Washington asked what he could do, Kosciusko said, "Try me." Washington made him a Colonel of Engineers, and Kosciusko helped build forts for the army for the rest of the war. In 1778, Casimir Pulaski also came from Poland. He helped organize new groups of soldiers and fought the British in the southern colonies. He was killed at the Battle of Savannah, Georgia, in 1779.

Military engineer Thadeusz (Thaddeus) Kosciusko came from Poland to help build fortifications for the Continental Army.

1778, Friedrich was an American citizen when he died in 1794. Since his death, his contributions have not been forgotten. Many American cities and towns, such as Steubenville, Ohio, are named for Friedrich Wilhelm von Steuben, honoring one of the most important generals in the American War of Independence.

GLOSSARY

alliance–when two or more countries are friendly, agree to help each other, and fight against common enemies.

allies–countries that agree to support one another when they are in need.

baron–title held by some members of the European upper class.

casualties–soldiers who are killed, wounded, or missing in battle.

Continentals–another name for American soldiers during the American War of Independence.

Continental Congress–legislature of the American colonists.

Continental Army–another name for the American army during the Revolutionary War.

French and Indian War (Seven Years' War)–conflict, which lasted from 1756 to 1763, between France, Great Britain, and several other European countries over control of North America.

general–highest ranking officer in the army.

Loyalists–colonists who supported King George III, opposed the Revolutionary War, and wanted to remain part of Great Britain.

marksmanship–ability to shoot a gun accurately.

militia–a group of civilians who volunteer to become soldiers in emergencies.

musket–a type of rifle.

negotiations–discussions between two opposing sides in an effort to resolve their disagreement.

Parliament–the British government.

redcoats–nickname given to British soldiers because of the red coats they wore.

skirmishes–small battles fought in wars.

CHRONOLOGY

1730	Friedrich Wilhelm von Steuben is born on September 13 in Magdeburg, Prussia.
1746	Joins the Prussian army and is given the rank of lance corporal.
1756	The French and Indian War (Seven Years' War) begins.
1763	Great Britain and Prussia defeat France and its allies as the Seven Years' War ends; Friedrich is fired from his job in the Prussian army.
1777	Meets Benjamin Franklin and Silas Deane and travels to America to volunteer for the American War of Independence against Great Britain.
1778	Meets George Washington, who agrees to allow Friedrich to help train American soldiers at Valley Forge; appointed Inspector General of the American army and given the rank of major general; helps Americans defeat British army at Battle of Monmouth.
1778–1779	Writes a book called *Regulations for the Order and Discipline of the Troops of the United States.*
1780	Named commander of Continental Army in Virginia.
1781	American and French forces defeat British at Battle of Yorktown.
1783	The Treaty of Paris is signed, ending the American Revolutionary War and creating the independent United States of America.
1784	Resigns from the American army.
1789	Builds log cabin in Utica, New York.
1794	Moves from New York City to Utica where he dies on November 29.

REVOLUTIONARY WAR TIME LINE —

1765   The Stamp Act is passed by the British. Violent protests against it break out in the colonies.

1766   Britain ends the Stamp Act.

1767   Britain passes a law that taxes glass, painter's lead, paper, and tea in the colonies.

1770   Five colonists are killed by British soldiers in the Boston Massacre.

1773   People are angry about the taxes on tea. They throw boxes of tea from ships in Boston harbor into the water. It ruins the tea. The event is called the Boston Tea Party.

1774   The British pass laws to punish Boston for the Boston Tea Party. They close Boston harbor. Leaders in the colonies meet to plan a response to these actions.

1775   The battles of Lexington and Concord begin the American Revolution.

1776   The Declaration of Independence is signed. France and Spain give money to help the Americans fight Britain. Nathan Hale is captured by the British. He is charged with being a spy and is executed.

1777   Leaders choose a flag for America. The American troops win some important battles over the British. General Washington and his troops spend a very cold, hungry winter in Valley Forge.

1778   France sends ships to help the Americans win the war. The British are forced to leave Philadelphia.

1779	French ships head back to France. The French support the Americans in other ways.
1780	Americans discover that Benedict Arnold is a traitor. He escapes to the British. Major battles take place in North and South Carolina.
1781	The British surrender at Yorktown.
1783	A peace treaty is signed in France. British troops leave New York.
1787	The U.S. Constitution is written. Delaware becomes the first state in the Union.
1789	George Washington becomes the first president. John Adams is vice president.

FURTHER READING ═══════

Barner, Bob. *Which Way to the Revolution? A Book About Maps.* New York: Holiday House, 1998.

Draper, Allison Stark. *What People Wore During the American Revolution.* New York: PowerKids Press, 2000.

Holmes, Richard. *Eyewitness: Battle.* New York: DK Publishing, 2000.

Moore, Kay. *If You Lived at the Time of the American Revolution.* New York: Scholastic, 1998.

Quackenbush, Robert M. *Daughter of Liberty—A True Story of the American Revolution.* New York: Hyperion, 1999.

PICTURE CREDITS ═══════

INDEX

ABOUT THE AUTHOR

BRUCE ADELSON has written 12 books for adults and children, including *Brushing Back Jim Crow—The Integration of Minor League Baseball in the American South* and *The Composite Guide to Field Hockey,* as well as three other historical biographies for children. A former elementary school substitute teacher and former commentator for National Public Radio and CBS Radio, Bruce is currently a book/multimedia reviewer for Children's Literature, a practicing attorney, and the proud father of Michael Daniel who was born in April 2001.

Senior Consulting Editor **ARTHUR M. SCHLESINGER, JR.** is the leading American historian of our time. He won the Pulitzer Prize for his book *The Age of Jackson* (1945), and again for *A Thousand Days* (1965). This chronicle of the Kennedy Administration also won a National Book Award. He has written many other books, including a multi-volume series, *The Age of Roosevelt.* Professor Schlesinger is the Albert Schweitzer Professor of the Humanities at the City University of New York, and has been involved in several other Chelsea House projects, including the Colonial Leaders series of biographies on the most prominent figures of early American history.

> **Dedication**: This book is dedicated to Michael Daniel Adelson, who was born as this book was being completed. May your life be filled with joy, love, and many, many books.